ENCYCLOPEDIAS FOR KIDS

THE HORSE

ENCYCLOPEDIA FOR KIDS

BY ETHAN PEMBROKE

Abdo Reference

An Imprint of Abdo Publishing
abdobooks.com

TABLE OF CONTENTS

HORSE DIAGRAM

There are many terms used to describe a horse's unique body. Knowing these terms can give people context when they are learning about horses. For example, knowing where a horse's withers are will help people understand where the height of a horse is measured.

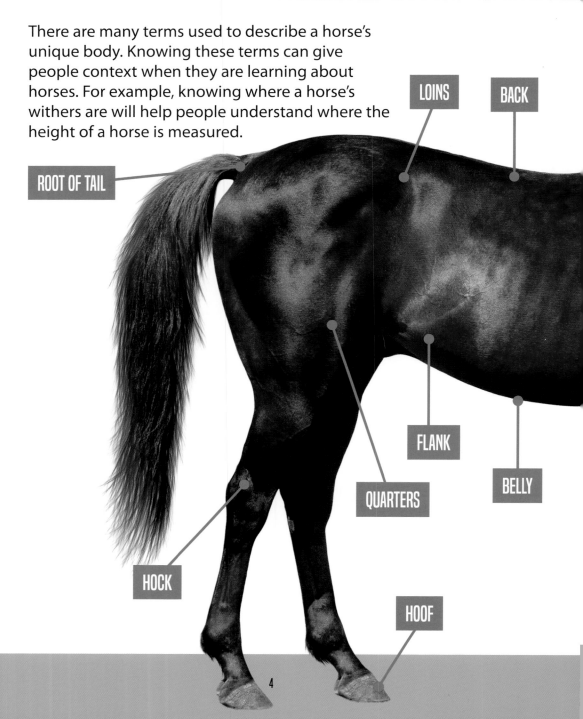

LOINS

BACK

ROOT OF TAIL

FLANK

QUARTERS

BELLY

HOCK

HOOF

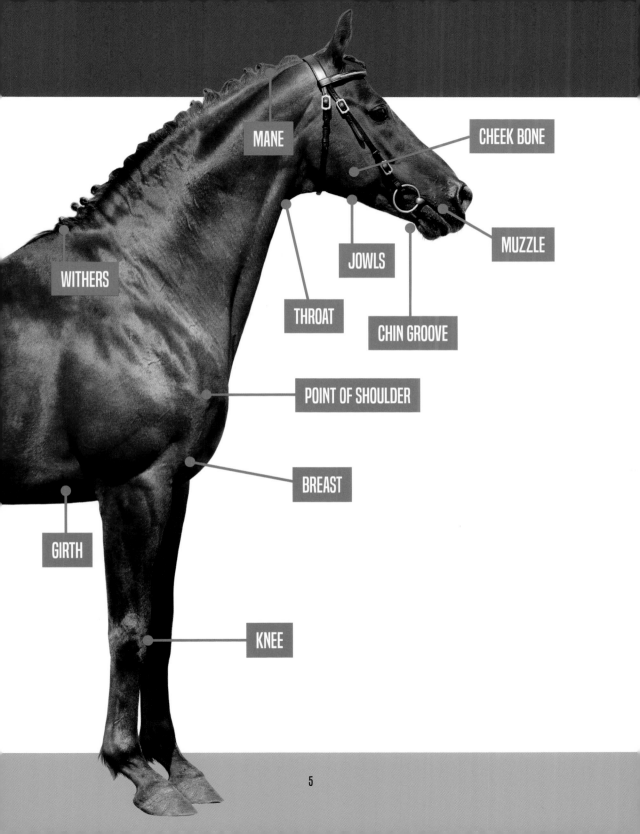

MANE

CHEEK BONE

WITHERS

JOWLS

THROAT

CHIN GROOVE

MUZZLE

POINT OF SHOULDER

BREAST

GIRTH

KNEE

COAT COLORS AND PATTERNS

Horses come in many different colors and patterns. Some common ones include bay, buckskin, chestnut, dun, palomino, pinto, and roan.

BAY

Bay coats are reddish brown. These horses will also have black tails, manes, and lower limbs.

BUCKSKIN

Buckskin coats are golden, and the horses should have black markings on the legs and ears. They also have black tails and manes.

CHESTNUT

Chestnut horses can have light- to dark-red coats. Their manes and tails can sometimes be lighter than their coats.

DUN

Dun horses can have sandy-gray coats, though they range in shade. Duns have a dorsal stripe running along their backs, ears that are tipped in dark coloring, and cobwebbing on their coats.

PALOMINO

Palomino is a golden coat color. Palomino horses have tails and manes that are always lighter than the body coat color.

PINTO

Horses with pinto patterns appear to have paint splattered on them. They can have either white splatters on a colored body, or colored splatters over a white body.

ROAN

Horses that have roan patterning can have a base color of bay, chestnut, black, or more. What distinguishes these horses as roan is the white hairs mixed in with the colored hairs.

HORSE TYPES AND BREEDS

Horses can be organized into three categories: draft horses, light horses, and ponies. These categories are based on how big the animal is. Horses are measured in 4-inch (10-cm) units called hands. This measurement is taken from the top of the withers to the ground.

Paint horse

Shetland ponies

DRAFT HORSES

Draft horses are heavy, muscular, and large. They were bred to pull weighty loads. They can weigh between 1,400 to 2,200 pounds (635 to 1,000 kg) or more and stand 16 to 19 hands high.

Starting in the 1830s, draft horses were brought from Europe to North America to help with agriculture. These strong, well-built horses pulled heavy equipment to help farmers with their harvests. Sometimes, more than 40 of these horses would be harnessed to one machine. Today, draft horses can still be found on farms. They are used for many tasks such as pulling carriages in parades, helping clear fallen trees in forests, and carrying riders. Clydesdale horses are one type of draft horse.

BELGIAN HORSES

Belgian horses have short legs and large muscles. They stand 16 to 17 hands high and can weigh between 1,800 and 2,200 pounds (820 to 1,000 kg). Belgians can be many colors, including roan, bay, sorrel, or chestnut.

Belgian horse

Percheron horse

PERCHERON HORSES

Percheron horses have long, thin ears and wide foreheads. They have long necks and stand around 15 to 19 hands high. These horses weigh around 1,800 to 2,600 pounds (815 to 1,180 kg). They can have a bay, sorrel, roan, black, chestnut, or gray coloring.

SHIRE HORSES

Shire horses have feathering on the lower part of their legs. Stallions of this breed can stand around 16 to 17 hands high and weigh 2,200 pounds (1,000 kg). Shire horses can be black, gray, brown, or bay.

Shire horse

LIGHT HORSES

Light horses are quick, and these long-legged animals can be used for racing, showing, or riding. They can be 12 to 17 hands high and can weigh between 900 to 1,400 pounds (400 to 635 kg). Many of today's breeds are light horses, including American paint horses, Arabians, quarter horses, and Thoroughbred horses. In addition, most mustangs, palomino horses, and pinto horses are in this group. Some people put miniature horses into this category, while others say they belong in the pony class.

There are various horse types found in the light horse category, including stock, hunter, and saddle types. Stock horses are used for working on ranches and racing short distances. They are often muscular and have necks that are positioned forward instead of upward. Some stock horses include the quarter horse and paint horse.

Akhal-Teke
horse

Morgan
horse

Hunter type horses are also known as sport horses. They were bred to take riders long distances and have the athletic skills to leap over things such as fences. When compared with stock horses, hunter types have longer legs and a leaner body. Thoroughbreds are one type of hunter horse.

Saddle horses have been bred for showing and for pleasure riding. These horses have long legs, and their feet lift high when they walk. Arabians are one type of saddle horse. They were developed as desert riding horses. Arabians are now commonly used for shows.

AKHAL-TEKE HORSE

Akhal-Teke horses have a lot of speed and endurance. These horses can be around 14 to 16 hands high and weigh between 900 to 1,000 pounds (410 to 450 kg). Akhal-Teke horses can be bay, black, gray, or red.

MORGAN HORSE

The Morgan horse is known for its stamina. This breed stands around 14 to 15 hands high and weighs around 900 to 1,100 pounds (400 to 500 kg). Morgan horses are often solid colors such as chestnut, black, or bay.

PONIES

Ponies are small, reaching less than 14.2 hands high. They are used for transporting light loads and can be ridden. Some ponies include Highlands and Shetlands.

Ponies reach maturity faster than horses do. They also have thicker tails and manes, and they have shorter legs when compared with horses. In addition, ponies often have longer lifespans than horses. They are known for their endurance and good natures.

CONNEMARA PONY

Connemara ponies come from Ireland and can be used for riding and in shows. These ponies are around 12.2 to 14.2 hands high and weigh around 600 pounds (270 kg). They can be many different colors.

Connemara pony

Dartmoor pony

DARTMOOR PONY

Dartmoor ponies are good mounts for kids. These animals are around 12 hands high and weigh about 440 pounds (200 kg). Dartmoors can be many colors, including bay, brown, or black.

WELSH PONY AND COB

Welsh ponies and cobs are smart and usually have good attitudes. These ponies stand around 12 hands high, but can sometimes be taller. They weigh around 500 pounds (225 kg). The ponies can be chestnut, black, bay, gray, cream, or roan.

Welsh cob

BREED HISTORY

Horses are strong and beautiful creatures. They descend from a small animal called eohippus that lived more than 55 million years ago. But horses have changed much since then.

Humans and horses have been companions for hundreds of years. Before cars and trains, horseback was the fastest way to travel on land. Horses have helped people farm, settle land, deliver mail, and fight in wars.

Horses, such as American paint horses, are built for running and working.

A paint horse's markings make it easy to distinguish from many other breeds.

Spaniards brought horses to North America in the 1500s. Before that time, most Native Americans had never seen these animals. However, horses soon became an important part of their lives.

American paint horses were especially treasured. This is still true today. Many people enjoy riding, racing, and working with these specially colored horses.

APPEARANCE

American paint horses come in a variety of patterns and colors. They have strong bones and are well balanced. Their heads and necks display grace and elegance.

The American paint horse has a body that is perfect for ranch work. A paint horse's hindquarters are made of strong muscles. They have broad chests and a stock horse body type. An average paint horse stands 14.2 to 16 hands high.

The American Paint Horse Association (APHA) was created to preserve and promote the paint horse. The APHA is the second-largest breed registry in the United States. It has strict guidelines that each horse must meet in order to be registered as an American paint horse.

AMERICAN PAINT HORSE SIZE

6 FEET
(1.8 M)

15 HANDS HIGH
(5 FEET / 1.5 M)

Horses need a lot of room to graze.

COLOR

An American paint horse's main feature is its colorful coat. It has white splotches on any color. These colors include black, bay, brown, chestnut, dun, sorrel, palomino, buckskin, gray, or roan. The various colors can form three specific coat patterns.

A paint horse with the tobiano pattern has large spots of color with smooth edges. There is usually some white on the horse's back. The horse's head is either a solid color or has a blaze, a star, or a strip of color. All four legs are usually white below the knees. Its tail is usually two colors.

No two paint horse coat patterns are exactly alike.

This paint horse displays the blaze face marking.

The overo-patterned horse has at least one dark-colored leg. Distinctive markings appear on its head and face. The markings are unusual and scattered. The horse's tail is usually just one color.

White marks don't often appear between the withers and the tail. A paint horse with the tovero pattern has characteristics of both the tobiano and overo. At least one of the eyes is blue.

Paint horses are bred for their color patterns.

WHAT MAKES THEM SPECIAL

American paint horses descended from horses brought to North America by Spaniards. Many of these animals escaped and formed herds of wild horses. They roamed the prairies and deserts of the western United States.

Paint horses tend to be friendly.

Paint horses have lots of stamina and speed.

Cowboys tamed paint horses. They found that this breed worked well with cattle. So, it became a strong, dependable ranch horse.

Over time, breeding has improved the athletic ability of paint horses. They are sturdy, intelligent, and willing animals. Paint horses are good for both ranch work and pleasure riding. They are also rodeo horses and show horses. They are even friendly with children.

FOALS

A baby horse is called a foal. Horses are mammals, which means their foals are born live. Having one foal at a time is most common. The mother is usually pregnant for about 11 months.

Within an hour of being born, a foal will stand for the first time. It may wobble on its long, skinny legs. Its mother will help it to start drinking her milk. By instinct, a foal will follow its mother. A foal can trot and gallop within 24 hours. However, it will tire easily, so it needs a lot of rest.

A foal drinks its mother's milk and eats grass for about two months. After this time, it may start to share its mother's feed. When the American paint horse foal is four and a half to six months old, it is weaned from its mother.

Around 40,000 American paint foals are registered with the APHA every year.

Breeders study genetics when they want to breed a foal with a certain coat.

TRAINING

Training begins soon after a foal's birth. The young foal will slowly become accustomed to people. As it grows, it will learn to wear a halter. After one year, it can be trained to wear a saddle.

Horses are creatures of habit. They learn every time they are ridden. When training, the teacher always uses the same words in the same tone of voice.

A trainer teaches a horse through conditioning. For example, a trainer sitting on a horse might squeeze his or her legs. The trainer

Halters are used to tie a horse up, lead a horse, or keep a horse from wandering away.

continues this action until the horse gives the desired response. Then the horse is rewarded.

The horse learns how to move from these signals. When a horse has learned to follow signals, it can learn more complicated activities.

Paint horses are trained for many purposes. They work on ranches or as trail mounts. No matter what its training, this amazing breed is a favorite of many people throughout the world.

Foals aren't the only ones who need training. Riders should learn how to properly treat a horse.

Paint horses are known for their trainability.

BREED HISTORY

The Arabian is one of the oldest modern horse breeds. It first appeared more than 2,000 years ago. At that time, it was established on the Arabian Peninsula in the Middle East. Starting in the 1700s, the breed spread to Europe. Arabians were first bred in the United States in 1888.

Arabian horses have been used to breed other types of light horses.

An Arabian horse's hardiness can be traced back to its origins in harsh desert conditions.

APPEARANCE

The Arabian horse is considered unmatched in its beauty. Its head is unmistakable. The wide-set eyes are large and dark. A broad forehead tapers to a narrow muzzle with large nostrils. From the side, the face appears to scoop in above the nose.

A high, arched neck is another mark of an Arabian. The horse has a long, silky mane and tail. The tail is held high.

Arabian horses weigh an average of 800 to 1,000 pounds (360 to 450 kg). They stand about 15 hands high.

ARABIAN HORSE SIZE

6 FEET
(1.8 M)

15 HANDS HIGH
(5 FEET / 1.5 M)

Arabians have a distinct head shape.

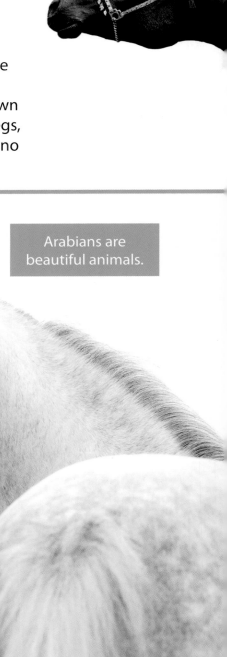

COLOR

Arabians are solid-colored horses. They can be gray, bay, chestnut, black, or roan. Gray horses are born dark and become gray and even white with age.

A bay horse has a light to dark reddish-brown coat with black points. Points are the horse's legs, mane, and tail. A horse with a brown coat and no black points is a chestnut.

Arabians are beautiful animals.

34

Almost all Arabian horses have black skin under their coats. This dark coloring helps to protect the horses from the hot desert sun.

Black horses have black coats and points. Roan horses have white hairs mixed with bay, chestnut, or black hairs. Roan coloring is rare among Arabians.

Arabians can have white markings on the head and the legs. Head markings include a bald face, a star, a stripe, a blaze, and a snip. Leg markings may be a coronet, a sock, or a stocking.

Daily grooming helps keep the Arabian's coat healthy and clean. Owners need a rubber currycomb to remove dirt from the horse's coat. A body brush cleans the Arabian's skin. Owners should use sponges to clean the horse's face and under its tail.

Arabians should have their teeth checked once a year.

The desert can be a difficult place to live.

WHAT MAKES THEM SPECIAL

The deserts of the Middle East are windy, dry, and vast. Over time, Arabian horses adapted to these harsh conditions. They grew into horses known for speed and strength.

Today, Arabians compete in many sports. These include racing and endurance riding. No other breed can run long distances like the Arabian.

Jockeys take horse races very seriously.

In addition to its abilities, the Arabian has a good disposition. It is gentle, affectionate, and loves to be around people. The Arabian is also courageous and loyal.

Today, Arabian horses are well loved. Many other horses are bred with Arabians for improved speed, endurance, and spirit. For example, Arabians helped to develop the Thoroughbred racehorse.

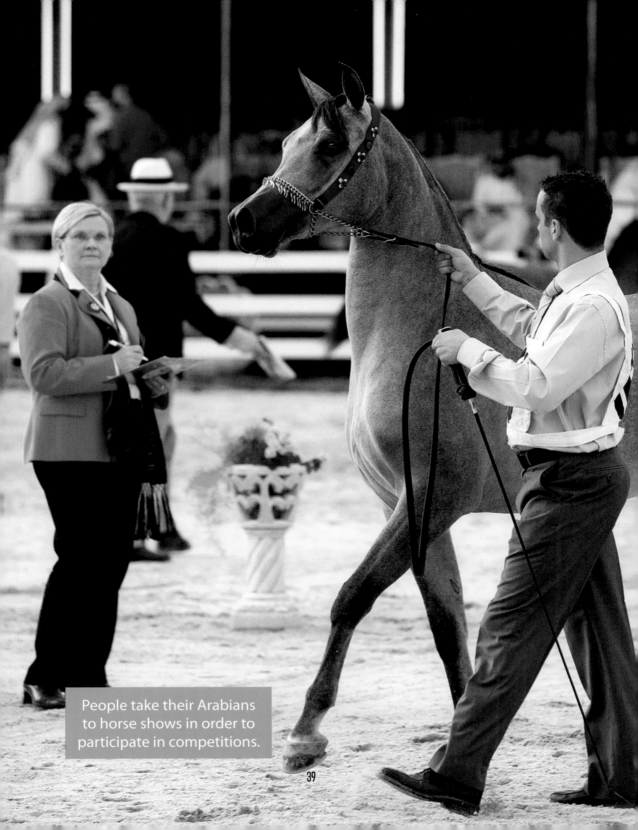

People take their Arabians to horse shows in order to participate in competitions.

FOALS

An Arabian foal may take its first wobbly steps a few minutes after birth. Within the first hour, it will start drinking its mother's milk.

A foal can gallop beside its mother soon after being born.

40

Arabians move in a fluid motion.

An Arabian foal is weaned when it is four or five months old. Then, it spends its time growing and playing with other young horses. They learn how to jump, run, and balance themselves.

TRAINING

Arabian horses are intelligent and eager to please. In fact, they learn more quickly than some other horse breeds.

Training an Arabian requires skill and patience. However, before training begins, an Arabian foal must learn to wear some of its tack. First, the foal adjusts to a head collar called a halter. As it grows, the foal begins to accept handling from a person.

Arabian horses are best suited for experienced riders and owners.

Lunge lining is when a person holds a long rein and the horse moves in circles around him or her.

In its second year, the Arabian begins training on a long rein called a lunge line. The horse also learns to wear a bit. Next, the horse learns to wear a saddle. But an Arabian should not be ridden until it is around three years old. That's because it is still developing and the weight of a rider could hurt it.

Properly trained Arabian horses can perform many sports or jobs. This beautiful breed is sure to stay popular with horse lovers for years to come.

CLYDESDALE HORSES

BREED HISTORY

During the 1700s, Clydesdales were developed in Scotland for farming. They were named for the River Clyde near Lanarkshire. The Clydesdale was introduced to the United States in 1842.

In the late 1800s, Clydesdales in the United States were used to pull wagons, power machines, and work on farms.

Clydesdale horses are strong enough to pull a plow in a farm field.

APPEARANCE

Clydesdale horses are not dainty. They weigh from 1,600 to 2,400 pounds (725 to 1,000 kg). Clydesdales also stand between 16 and 18 hands high.

To match its huge body, a Clydesdale has a long neck and a large head. The horse's face is flat and broad.

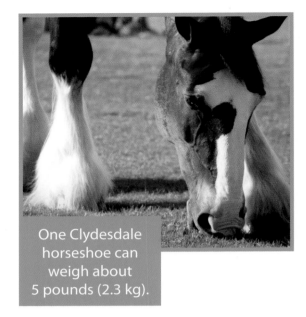

One Clydesdale horseshoe can weigh about 5 pounds (2.3 kg).

CLYDESDALE HORSE SIZE

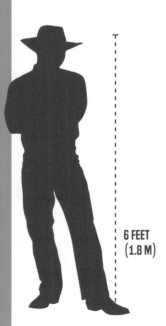

6 FEET (1.8 M)

17 HANDS HIGH (5.6 FEET / 1.7 M)

Clydesdales are a very recognizable draft horse breed.

One of the Clydesdale's most recognizable features is its legs. Below the knees and hocks, the legs have feathering. This long hair grows to the ground.

Under a Clydesdale's feathering hide large, round hooves. When the horse walks, it lifts its hooves high off the ground. These hooves are very big compared to a racehorse's hooves, which are about one-quarter of the size of a Clydesdale's. The large hooves help carry the horse's weight.

COLOR

Most Clydesdale horses are bay, chestnut, or black in color. Clydesdales can also be roan. Roan horses have white hairs mixed in with one of the other colors.

Bay is the most common coat color for Clydesdales. Bay horses have light to dark reddish-brown bodies with black points.

A chestnut horse also has a brown coat but without black points. Brown horses have brown and black coat hairs with black points. Black horses have all black hairs.

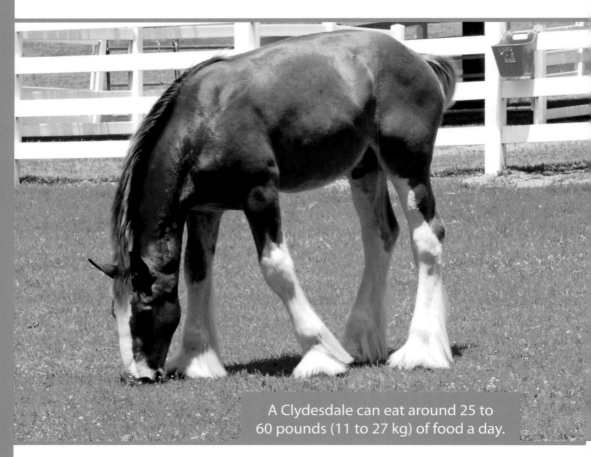

A Clydesdale can eat around 25 to 60 pounds (11 to 27 kg) of food a day.

Blaze face markings can cover a large part of the horse's nose.

A Clydesdale has white markings on its head and legs. A large strip usually runs down the center of its face. This is either a bald face or a blaze. Leg markings can be socks or stockings.

Some Clydesdale horses have white body markings. Clydesdales can have any mix of head, leg, and body markings.

WHAT MAKES THEM SPECIAL

Clydesdales belong to a group known as draft horses. They were originally bred to carry knights in armor. Later, Clydesdales were used as draft horses. Draft horses help plow land and haul heavy loads.

In the United States, most Clydesdales became city horses. Instead of plowing land, they pulled carriages. They were also seen in parades and competitions.

In the past, companies used Clydesdale horses to pull wagons advertising their products. This tradition continues.

Good qualities for a draft horse include strength and calmness.

Horses can do well in parades if trained properly.

FOALS

A healthy Clydesdale foal weighs between 110 and 180 pounds (50 and 80 kg). Once the foal is standing, it begins to nurse. Clydesdale foals are weaned when they are about five months old. Most Clydesdales live about 20 to 25 years.

Every year, about 600 Clydesdales are registered in the United States.

For the first few months after its birth, a Clydesdale foal can gain around 4 pounds (1.8 kg) each day.

Clydesdales are known to work well with riders of all levels of experience.

TRAINING

Clydesdale horses can be trained for many uses. These include driving, riding, and competition. Training for driving begins at two years of age. A Clydesdale is introduced to the harness gradually. Then, it learns to pull a cart.

The Clydesdale can then be trained to work with a team. Teams are made up of pairs of horses. A new team member is paired with an experienced one. This teaches the new Clydesdale how to be part of a pair.

Each pair has a different role. The lead horses are hitched at the front of the team. The wheel horses are closest to the wagon. They are the strongest and do most of the pulling. Swing and body horses are hitched between these pairs.

A Clydesdale's harness should fit well. Each one weighs about 130 pounds (59 kg).

Clydesdale horses are an amazing breed. They are huge, powerful animals. They are also beautiful and noble. It's no wonder these famous horses are known as gentle giants.

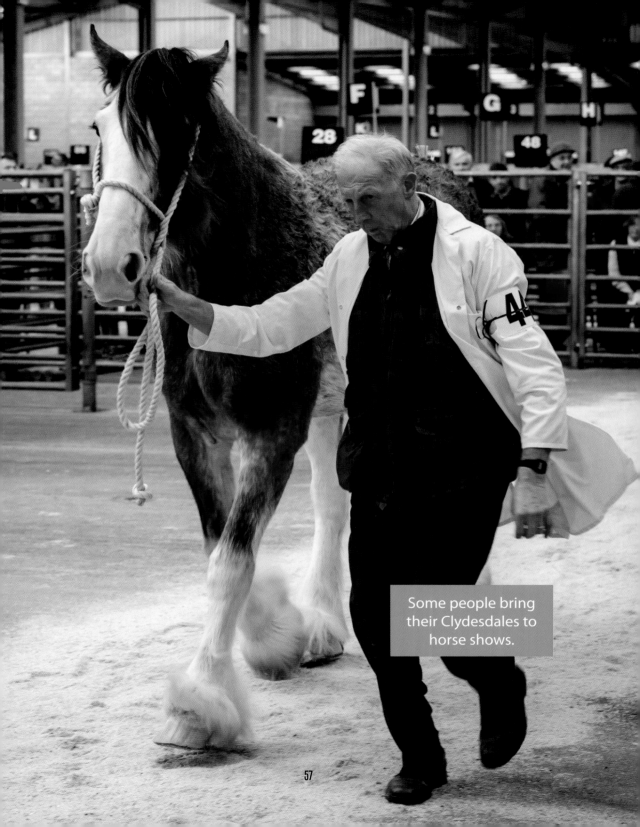

Some people bring their Clydesdales to horse shows.

57

HIGHLAND PONIES

BREED HISTORY

Ponies and horses have similar features and can do many similar things. But there are a few differences. The main differences between horses and ponies are size and character. A pony's legs are short compared to its body. A pony is 14.2 hands high or less.

One of the best-known ponies is the Highland pony. It is appreciated for its sturdiness. Highland pony bloodlines can be traced to the 1830s. These animals are still popular today.

A Highland pony's eyes are closer together than a lot of other breeds' eyes. That allows the pony to have good frontal vision.

Highland ponies are popular with pony lovers all around Scotland, England, and other parts of the British Isles.

APPEARANCE

Experts recognize a Highland pony by its distinct features. For example, this pony has a wide forehead. The distance between the eyes and muzzle is short. The nostrils are wide. And the pony has a strong neck.

A Highland pony is about 13 to 14.2 hands high. This pony's body is compact. Its hindquarters are very strong. It also has sturdy feet, so it can travel easily over rough or marshy ground.

This breed has short legs with wide knees. The feathery hair on the back of the legs is soft and silky. The tail and mane are flowing and are often left untrimmed.

HIGHLAND PONY SIZE

6 FEET
(1.8 M)

13 HANDS HIGH
(4.3 FEET / 1.3 M)

Highland ponies are known for their quiet natures.

COLOR

A Highland pony can be any of a wide assortment of colors. The coat may be liver chestnut, gray, black, brown, or bay. Highlands also come in a variety of duns, such as mouse, yellow, gray, and cream.

Many Highland ponies have a narrow stripe of color along the top of their backs. They may also have stripes similar to a zebra's on their legs. Highland ponies should not have any white markings. However, some have a small star on the forehead.

Highland ponies are the biggest of Britain's native pony breeds.

In the 1700s, Highland ponies were smaller than they are today.

Some Highland ponies get so dirty that people cannot tell what color they are. Still, grass-kept ponies do not need to be groomed every day. Mud keeps the skin and coat in good condition. But daily grooming pleases a stabled pony and is a form of massage.

Highlands have long, flowing manes.

WHAT MAKES THEM SPECIAL

The Highland pony is native to the mountains of Scotland. It is able to do many different jobs. Crofters, or small farmers, originally used these ponies to pull carts. Often, Highland ponies were used as pack animals before roads were built.

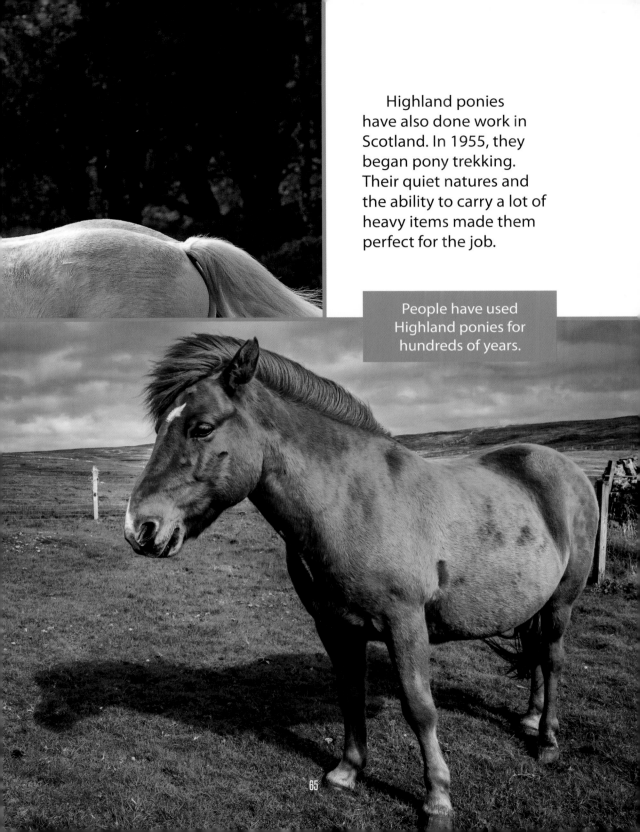

Highland ponies have also done work in Scotland. In 1955, they began pony trekking. Their quiet natures and the ability to carry a lot of heavy items made them perfect for the job.

People have used Highland ponies for hundreds of years.

There are few Highland ponies in the United States. Most are in Europe.

Today, Highland ponies still work in the hills of Scotland. They are used for riding and driving. And they are good family ponies. Highlands are a favorite pony for many people.

A Highland's thick coat and facial hair help protect it in the winter.

FOALS

A female Highland pony is pregnant for about 11 months. When she's ready to give birth, she needs a comfortable, private place. Most often, she has just one foal.

A Highland foal should soon start drinking its mother's milk. This milk has a lot of vitamins and other things a foal needs. Within a few hours, the foal will stand on its wobbly legs. By instinct, the foal follows its mother.

There are between 5,000 and 6,000 Highland ponies around today.

A Highland foal's color can change as it gets older.

Soon, the foal will be running and playing. A young Highland pony will want to trot and gallop. It uses up its energy quickly by playing. So the foal needs to rest often.

TRAINING

A Highland pony begins its training right after it is born. Its very first lesson is getting used to people. It must learn to allow humans to work with it.

The trainer will teach the pony slowly and patiently. When it is a few days old, the trainer will introduce the pony to a halter. This is an important first step. When it is two years old, the pony may get used to a saddle.

Some Highland pony competitions are held in the United Kingdom.

With the right training, a Highland pony can even help hunters bring game in from the field.

At about three years old, the pony should start training on a lunge line. The pony will be on one end with the trainer on the other end. The pony will learn to follow voice commands.

Once the pony is disciplined, it will learn to tolerate a rider on its back. The trainer will slowly introduce physical commands that go with voice commands.

Once a pony learns signals, it can be trained for a certain task. Many Highlands still trek and perform farmwork in the hills of Scotland. However, some people around the world enjoy riding and showing them as well.

MINIATURE HORSES

BREED HISTORY

Throughout the years, many people have bred horses. This resulted in many different horse types. Different features, such as muscle strength, were improved through breeding.

   One special breed is the miniature horse. This tiny horse has been bred for more than 400 years. Miniature horses are curious and intelligent. They love attention and are both gentle and affectionate, so they make good companions for all ages.

Miniature horses look like their large-breed cousins.

Miniature horses can live longer than other breeds.

APPEARANCE

The miniature horse is a breed based on height. Adult miniatures typically cannot be taller than 8.4 hands high. They weigh between 150 and 250 pounds (70 and 110 kg). They are not ponies. They are tiny horses with the same proportions as larger horses.

Miniature horses are bred with one main objective. A breeder's goal is to create the smallest possible perfect horse. All of the miniature's body parts are in proportion to one another.

MINIATURE HORSE SIZE

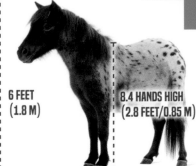

Miniature horses are more likely to get certain health problems, such as obesity, than the larger breeds.

6 FEET
(1.8 M)

8.4 HANDS HIGH
(2.8 FEET/0.85 M)

Some European royalty kept miniatures as pets. For example, in the 1650s, King Louis XIV of France had some.

It's easy to tell the difference between a horse and a miniature horse.

Miniature horses have well-muscled bodies. Their foreheads are broad, and they have large, wide-set eyes. The distance between the eyes and the muzzle is short. Miniature horses have long, flexible necks. And their ears are pointed and curve slightly inward.

Miniature horses are loved for their sizes. It is easier to transport miniatures than full-size horses. Miniatures can fit in station wagons, vans, pickup trucks, and horse trailers. They have even ridden as extra baggage in the cargo bay of an airplane.

COLOR

Miniature horses come in all typical horse colors. Basic coat colors and patterns include bay, dun, chestnut, brown, gray, and roan. The color of a horse is determined by more than the coat color. Skin, mane, tail, and leg coloring must all be taken into account, too.

Many people like miniature horses because they look like larger breeds but are much smaller and can be easier to handle.

Miniatures horses should be kept in a pasture away from larger horses.

Miniature horses can have any marking pattern. They can have leg or face markings. Face markings can be a star, a snip, a stripe, a blaze, or a freckled stripe. Miniatures can also have any eye color.

Regular grooming keeps a horse's coat healthy. Grooming pleases miniature horses and improves their appearance. They must be brushed daily to remove dirt and allow their coats to shine. Common grooming tools are a currycomb, a body brush, and a mane and tail comb.

Miniatures need room to run.

WHAT MAKES THEM SPECIAL

Miniature horses have a broad background. They developed from different breeds. Miniatures have ancestors who were Shetland ponies, Falabellas, and others.

Often, tiny horses were gathered together to do specific types of work. Many worked in coal mines in northern Europe. Miniature horses were chosen for this job because of their small sizes and the ability to pull heavy loads.

European nobles soon saw these tiny horses as something special. Around the 1600s, miniature horses were noble pets. By 1765, these horses were the subject of paintings and articles.

Many people bred these horses. In the 1900s, Lady Estella Hope, who lived in England, and her sisters began breeding miniature horses. They continued into the mid-1900s. Today, many of the smallest miniatures in the United States are descendants of this line.

Many horse colors have developed from years of breeding horses.

Trained horse veterinarians can help people keep their horses healthy.

FOALS

A miniature foal is tiny, standing only about 4 to 5.25 hands high at birth. It will soon start drinking its mother's milk.

Miniature horses only eat about 2 to 4 pounds (0.9 to 1.8 kg) of food every day.

For about two months, grass and the mare's milk should be enough food for the foal. Then, the foal should start sharing its mother's feed. When the foal is six months old, it will be weaned from its mother.

TRAINING

A miniature horse begins its training right after it is born. Its very first lesson is getting used to being with people. It must learn to allow humans to work with it.

Most horses have good memories. They should learn to respond to signals. Trainers must be patient and gentle when working with miniatures.

A miniature horse is not the best riding horse. It can only carry a person who weighs 70 pounds (32 kg) or less. However, it makes up for this by

Miniature horses can be trained to pull people in small carriages.

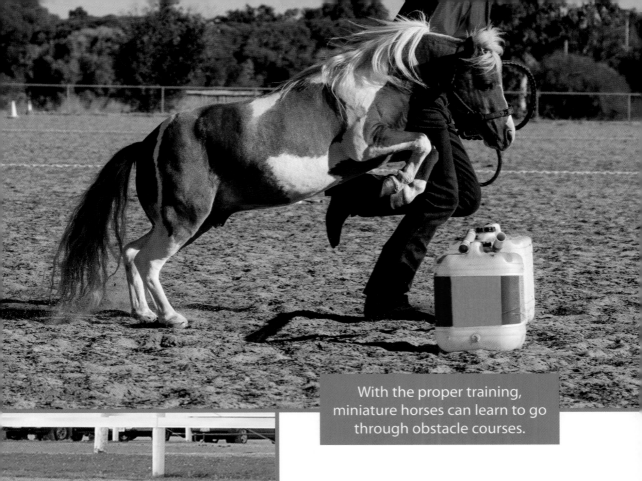

With the proper training, miniature horses can learn to go through obstacle courses.

being a good driving animal. When hooked up to a cart, it can easily pull one to two adults.

A miniature horse has the special talent of being a good therapy animal. It is often used in programs for elderly people, or for those with disabilities. It is even used by the Guide Horse Foundation as a guide for people who are blind.

MUSTANG HORSES

HISTORY

Spaniards first brought horses to the New World in the 1500s. Some of those horses escaped and started living in the wild. Today, descendants of those escaped horses are known as mustangs. This word comes from the Spanish word for a stray horse.

Mustang herds have foals, yearlings, mares, and a stallion.

Mustangs have well-built, muscular bodies.

APPEARANCE

Mustangs have a medium-sized body. An average mustang stands about 14.2 to 15.2 hands high. At this height, it weighs about 600 to 800 pounds (270 to 360 kg). However, some can be as short as 13 hands or as tall as 16 hands.

These horses have short backs, rounded rumps, and low-set tails. They have strong, hard feet. Their heads are broad with narrow faces. And their ears are short and curve toward each other.

MUSTANG HORSE SIZE

6 FEET
(1.8 M)

14.2 HANDS HIGH
(4.7 FEET / 1.4 M)

Mustangs have stocky legs, which makes them less likely to get injured.

COLOR

Mustangs come in a variety of colors, patterns, and sizes. Most often, mustangs are sorrel or bay in color. They can also be roan, black, white, paint, dun, or gray.

Mustang coats can have various spots, patches, and stripes.

There are different types of currycombs that people can use depending on their horses' needs.

Grooming helps keep a tamed mustang's coat healthy and looking nice. Brushing removes dirt and dandruff. If kept in a stable, mustangs should be groomed every day. This can be done with a body brush, a currycomb, and a mane and tail comb.

WHAT MAKES THEM SPECIAL

European settlers brought horses with them as they moved into the western United States. Some horses escaped or were turned loose by failed ranchers.

In the early 1900s, more than two million mustangs wandered the western United States. Ranchers valued these horses for their speed and endurance. Then, farming practices began to change. By the 1920s, tractors had replaced horses.

Wild mustangs live in states such as Wyoming, Montana, Utah, Idaho, New Mexico, Arizona, and more.

Wild mustangs must live off the land.

Horses living in the wild were soon seen as pests. The US government authorized removal of the horses, and people began killing them. Soon, fewer than 17,000 mustangs remained.

Sometimes, mustangs will fight with each other.

In 1971, the US Congress passed the Wild Free-Roaming Horse and Burro Act. This act protects, manages, and controls these animals. Today, about 39,000 wild horses roam the West.

The Bureau of Land Management monitors the sizes of mustang herds. Each year, thousands of wild horses are captured and put up for adoption.

FOALS

A mustang foal is born with long legs. It should stand within an hour of its birth. The foal will follow its mother around. In just a day, the foal will be running. But it uses up its energy quickly, so it needs a lot of rest.

For about two months, a mustang foal drinks its mother's milk and eats grass. Toward the end of that time, the captive foal should be sharing the mare's feed.

Mustangs usually give birth in the spring. That way, their foals have a better chance of being strong enough to survive the winter.

Mustang foals drink their mothers' milk to help them grow strong and healthy.

TRAINING

Training a mustang requires patience. These horses haven't been bred to be gentle with people for hundreds of years. Many also don't learn to trust people at a young age. So they are suspicious of people. It can take a while for mustangs to become used to humans.

Mustangs can be difficult to work with because of their independent natures.

With hard work, owners can train their mustangs and show them in events.

A trainer needs to gain a mustang's trust before the horse can be trained. Trainers use slow, calm movements with the horse. The trainers are tender but firm. Once trust is gained and the horse is gentled, a mustang can be trained.

Mustangs can compete in a variety of horse competitions.

HISTORY

The palomino horse has a long history. It has been around since horses were first domesticated. Most people believe the palomino descended from the Arabian horse.

Palominos are known for their beautiful golden coats.

Palominos came to North America in the 1500s. Spain's Queen Isabella sent six palominos to Mexico with Spanish explorers. Eventually, these golden horses spread north into present-day Texas and California.

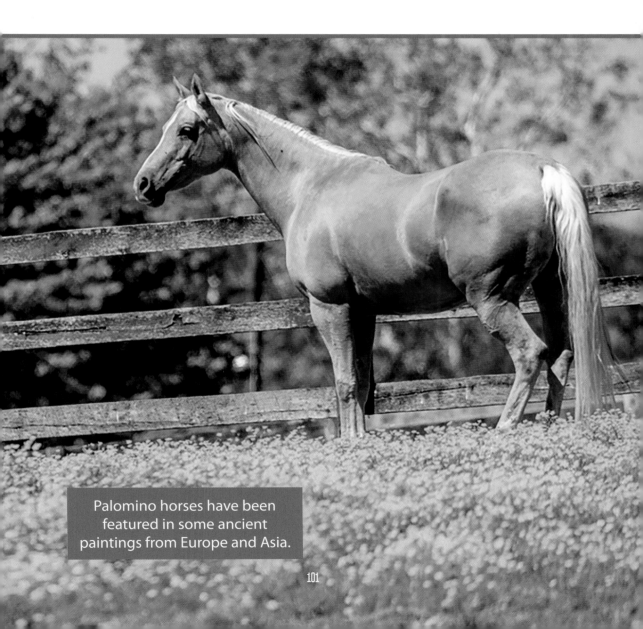

Palomino horses have been featured in some ancient paintings from Europe and Asia.

APPEARANCE

Palominos are not a true horse breed. Instead, they are a color type. A color type can occur in many different horse breeds.

A palomino's weight depends on what breed the horse is. Horse breeds are divided by size into three groups. They are light horses, heavy horses, and ponies. Most palomino horses are between 14 and 17 hands high.

Most palominos are classified as light horses. Breeds in this group usually weigh less than 1,300 pounds (590 kg). They are the best size for riding.

PALOMINO HORSE SIZE

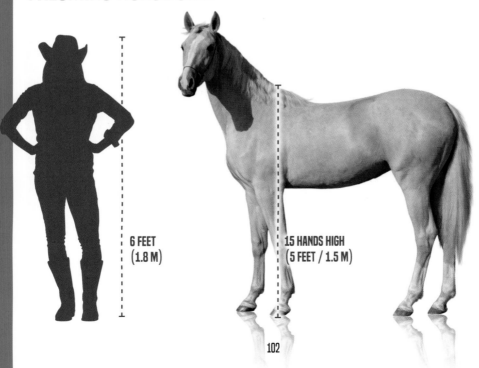

6 FEET
(1.8 M)

15 HANDS HIGH
(5 FEET / 1.5 M)

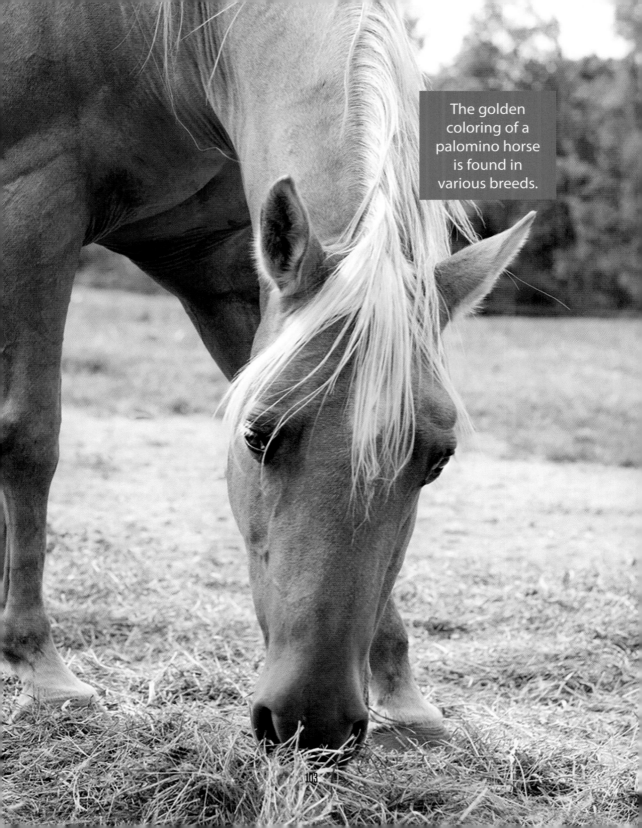

The golden coloring of a palomino horse is found in various breeds.

COLOR

The palomino is the true golden horse. The ideal coat is the color of a gold coin. In contrast to its golden coat, the palomino has dark skin. It has black, brown, or hazel eyes. The palomino's mane and tail are white or ivory. Palomino horses may have white markings on the head and the legs. The most common head markings are a star,

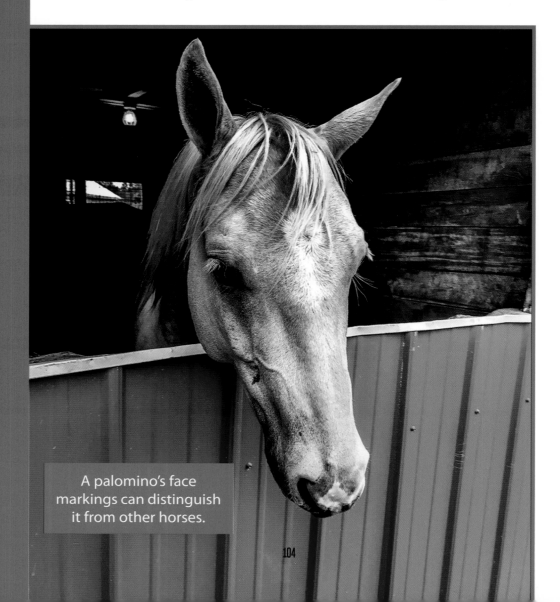

A palomino's face markings can distinguish it from other horses.

A palomino's light-colored mane and tail stand out against its golden body.

a stripe, a snip, a blaze, and a bald face. Common leg markings include ankles, socks, and stockings.

Since palominos are not a breed, reproducing their color is tricky. Breeding two palominos only produces palomino horses 50 percent of the time.

Horses grow a winter coat to keep them warm during the cold months.

The rest of the time, horses are born either chestnut or cremello. A chestnut horse has a reddish coat, mane, and tail. A cremello horse has a cream to light yellow coat. Breeding a chestnut with a cremello always produces a palomino.

WHAT MAKES THEM SPECIAL

People have enjoyed palomino horses for thousands of years. They were favorite horses of ancient emperors and kings. They were even represented in Greek myths.

Palominos have been used in parades, rodeos, and on trails.

Wild horses can have the palomino coloring.

Palominos can be various shades of gold.

In 1941, palomino lovers formed Palomino Horse Breeders of America (PHBA). This group keeps records of palominos and improves breeding standards.

The palomino color type can occur in every horse breed except the Thoroughbred. However, PHBA only registers palominos from select breeds. They are quarter horses, American saddlebreds, Arabian horses, Morgan horses, and Tennessee walking horses.

FOALS

Palominos develop quickly. After about six months, a foal no longer needs to nurse. At that time, it is weaned.

Young palominos spend the next few months with other young horses. Together they play, eat, and learn. Healthy palominos can live for 20 to 30 years.

Some people breed horses to try and get the palomino color.

Because palominos show up in many breeds, it's difficult to pin down a specific temperament for these horses.

TRAINING

Most palominos begin training at a young age. This helps the horses learn to trust people and take directions. One of the first lessons a palomino learns is to wear a halter.

Preparing a palomino to be ridden requires great skill and patience. Well-trained palominos can compete in many sports, such as jumping or barrel racing. Cowboys often use them for ranching. No matter its job, a palomino makes a wonderful companion for many years.

Training that is fun can make a palomino willing to learn and eager to please.

With the right training, palominos can be well suited for riders of any level.

PINTO HORSES

HISTORY

Spanish explorers brought pinto horses to North America in the 1500s. Eventually, pintos became an important part of American life. Farmers, ranchers, and travelers put them to work.

Pintos have a two-colored coat pattern.

In 1947, US pinto enthusiasts started the Pinto Horse Association of America (PHAA). Today, pinto horses are a popular choice for competitors as well as pleasure riders.

The Spanish word for paint is *pinto*.

APPEARANCE

Pintos are not a true horse breed. Instead, they are a color type. A color type horse is bred for its color or pattern. The color type may be displayed in many different breeds.

A pinto horse's shape and other body features depend on its breed. With so many breeds, pintos come in various sizes. Three sizes are miniature, pony, and horse.

Horses are measured from the ground up to their withers. At 8.5 hands high or fewer, miniature pintos are the smallest. Pinto ponies measure between 9.5 and 14 hands high. Most ponies weigh less than 800 pounds (360 kg).

The largest pinto size is the horse. These animals stand at least 14 hands high. Most pinto horses weigh up to 1,300 pounds (590 kg).

MINIATURE PINTO SIZE

6 FEET
(1.8 M)

8.5 HANDS HIGH
(2.8 FEET / 0.85 M)

PINTO PONY SIZE

6 FEET
(1.8 M)

12 HANDS HIGH
(4 FEET / 1.2 M)

PINTO HORSE SIZE

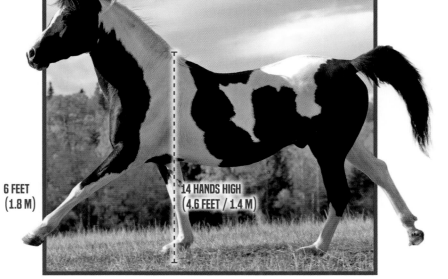

6 FEET
(1.8 M)

14 HANDS HIGH
(4.6 FEET / 1.4 M)

COLOR

The two recognized color combinations for pinto horses are piebald and skewbald. A black-and-white pinto displays the piebald coloring. A pinto with skewbald coloring is white with any color except black.

Overo and tobiano are the two color patterns for pintos. An overo pinto has a colored coat with white patches. The patches have jagged edges.

An overo's white spots never cross its back. This horse has a dark tail, mane, legs, and back. An overo commonly has a bald face marking on its head.

Skewbald coloring (*left*) and piebald coloring (*right*)

Overo color pattern

A tobiano pinto is a white horse with colored patches. The patches have smooth edges and may cross the horse's back.

A tobiano can have a two-tone mane and tail. All four legs are usually white below the knees and the hocks. Tobiano head markings include a star, a stripe, a snip, and a blaze.

WHAT MAKES THEM SPECIAL

After the Spanish brought horses to the New World, some Native American nations and tribes favored pinto horses for their colorings. Cowboys also valued these horses. Pintos could handle hard work and the rugged land of the West. In addition, every pinto coat was unique. The cowboys used the distinct coloring to identify individual horses.

The difference between pinto and paint horses is that pinto is a coloring, while paint is a breed. Many different breeds of horses can have pinto coloring.

Proper grooming, such as tail brushing, is important to keep horses looking their best.

Today, the PHAA registers many different horse breeds as pintos. Registered pintos are commonly quarter horses, Thoroughbreds, or Arabian horses. Other breeds include Morgans, American saddlebreds, and Tennessee walking horses.

FOALS

The pinto foal is born without teeth. As it grows older, it grows milk teeth. These are replaced with permanent teeth by age four or five.

After the foal is weaned, it joins other young horses. They sleep, eat, and play together. These activities help the young horses grow strong and healthy. Most horses live 25 to 30 years.

To have a tobiano foal, there must be a tobiano parent.

Foals needs lots of rest and nutrition to grow up healthy and strong.

TRAINING

Like all horses, a pinto learns most easily at a young age. One of the first lessons an owner must teach a pinto is how to wear a halter. This piece of tack fits over the foal's head like a collar. Soon after, the foal learns to lead on a rope. Leading is similar to how a dog walks on a leash.

Young riders should be educated and trained on how to take care of their horses.

Pinto horses should not be ridden until they are around three years old. Until that time, their bones are still growing. A human's weight could easily injure them.

Before riding occurs, a horse must be comfortable wearing a saddle. Once a pinto can safely be ridden, it can train for many different sports and jobs. With proper training, these colorful horses make great companions for any horse lover.

Saddles can range in weight from 10 to 60 pounds (4.5 to 27 kg).

HISTORY

In the 1800s, people weren't sure whether there were any truly wild horses left in the world. However, in the 1880s, Nikolay Przhevalsky reported finding herds of wild horses near the Gobi Desert in Asia.

After Przhevalsky's announcement, word spread that wild horses still existed. Rare animal collectors around the world soon wanted to capture the horses for their own. So, expeditions set out to catch Przewalski's (pshuh-VAHL-skeez) horses.

Przewalski's horses are the last species of wild horses in the world.

These horses are endangered due to hunting and loss of habitat.

Przewalski's horses remain popular attractions at zoos.

Capturing the shy horses was difficult. Full-grown horses were almost impossible to catch. But some of the expeditions succeeded in capturing foals.

Keeping the horses alive was a problem, but some of the horses survived. People discovered the wild animals could not be tamed. Still, they became prized objects for nobles and popular zoo attractions.

APPEARANCE

A Przewalski's horse is sturdy and compact. It stands 12 to 14 hands high. The Przewalski's neck is strong and short. The head is heavy with a long face. The eyes are dark and sit close to the ears.

This horse's mane and tail are dark. The mane hairs are stiff, so they stand upright. The hair stops between the ears, so there is no forelock. The tail hairs are short at the top of the tail. Lower down, they grow longer.

A Przewalski's horse is shy but highly alert. It has a shrill voice as well as excellent senses of hearing and smell. These traits all serve to protect it from danger.

PRZEWALSKI'S HORSE SIZE

6 FEET
(1.8 M)

13 HANDS HIGH
(4.3 FEET / 1.3 M)

Przewalski's horses grow thicker and longer coats in the winter to protect themselves from the cold.

COLOR

The Przewalski's coat is light brown, sandy, or reddish bay. Around the eyes, muzzle, and on the stomach, the coat is cream colored. A dark stripe runs down its back. Its lower legs are dark, or often have stripes similar to those of a zebra.

These horses have short, dark manes that shed every year.

Coats are palest near the stomach region in this species.

WHAT MAKES THEM SPECIAL

When Przewalski's horses were being captured, they were also being hunted. The animals were slowly killed off. Shortly after World War II (1939–1945), it appeared Przewalski's horses only existed in zoos.

But life was not easy in the zoos. The formerly wild horses did not have enough space. Sometimes, there wasn't enough grass. People also discovered that the horses were aggressive in captivity. They could not be handled or trained for riding.

In the wild, Przewalski's horses have a home range of up to 12 square miles (31 sq km).

Zoos breed Przewalski's horses and later release them with the hopes of increasing the wild population.

In addition, the zoos didn't trade the horses enough. So, the animals were forced to mate with their relatives. This made it more likely that foals would have diseases or defects.

Due to these problems, a captive Przewalski's life span was short. The number of pregnant mares also decreased and newborn foals did not always survive. Something needed to be done to save these horses from extinction.

If more Przewalski's horses are able to give birth while in captivity, that means more of these horses can eventually be released into the wild.

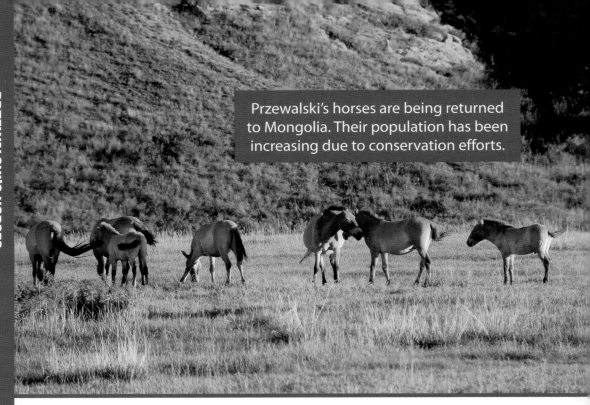

Przewalski's horses are being returned to Mongolia. Their population has been increasing due to conservation efforts.

Zoos changed their breeding practices. Some wanted to return Przewalski's horses to the wild. In 1977, three people in Rotterdam, Netherlands, created the Foundation for the Preservation and Protection of the Przewalski Horse (FPPPH). At that time, only about 300 Przewalski's horses were left.

The foundation created a plan to return the animals to the wild. In 1988, the foundation found a reserve in the steppes of Mongolia. The area is called Hustain Nuruu and is very similar to the Przewalski's original homeland. It became Hustai National Park, protecting both the land and the horses from outside influence.

FOALS

A Przewalski's mare starts having foals when she is about three years old. She is pregnant for about 11 to 12 months. In Mongolia, the birth season is around the end of May, June, and July.

A Przewalski's stallion starts looking for mating partners when he is about five years old. His instinct will be to create a group of mares. Often, he will wander until he finds another group with its own leader.

Przewalski's foals are able to walk and keep up with their herds 30 minutes after they are born.

At this point, the young stallion may fight the current leader. The fight may last days or sometimes weeks. If the young stallion is victorious, the mares must adjust to the new leader. Sometimes, the mares will leave the group and find another.

Przewalski's herds are made of several mares, a stallion, and foals. Bigger herds offer more protection against predators.

Stallions will fight each other to become the leader of a herd. Herds usually have no more than ten mares.

QUARTER HORSES

BREED HISTORY

In the 1500s, Spanish explorers left behind horses they had brought to North America. In about 1610, American colonists brought horses from England. They bred the Spanish horses with the English horses. The result was the quarter horse, which originated in about 1660.

Quarter horse races were a popular form of entertainment in colonial America. Colonists would place bets on which horse would win a quarter-mile race.

Quarter horses are fast sprinters. They can run up to 55 miles per hour (89 kmh) over a short distance.

The colonists used the new breed for transportation, farming, riding, and hunting. In Virginia and the Carolinas, the colonists also raced the horses. At the time, the breed was running quarter-mile races at high speeds. So it became known as the quarter horse.

APPEARANCE

A quarter horse has distinct features. The most important are its heavily muscled hindquarters. They give the horse a lot of power.

A quarter horse has a small muzzle and a short, wide head. Its neck is long and flexible. This breed's withers also hold a saddle easily.

An adult quarter horse stands between 14 and 16 hands high. Its weight is between 950 and 1,200 pounds (430 and 540 kg).

QUARTER HORSE SIZE

6 FEET
(1.8 M)

15 HANDS HIGH
(5 FEET / 1.5 M)

Quarter horses are known for being gentle and calm.

These horses have
muscular bodies
and hind legs.

COLOR

A quarter horse is often bay, sorrel, or chestnut colored. However, it can be any of 17 colors recognized by the American Quarter Horse Association (AQHA). The other colors include black, brown, buckskin, dun, red dun, gray, palomino, red roan, and blue roan.

Quarter horses come in many colors. They are usually solid in color, but some may have a few white markings on their faces and legs.

A quarter horse may have white markings on its face or lower legs, but nowhere else.

Daily grooming helps keep a quarter horse healthy and looking nice. Brushing removes dirt and sweat. A stabled horse should be groomed with a currycomb, a dandy brush, a body brush, and a mane comb.

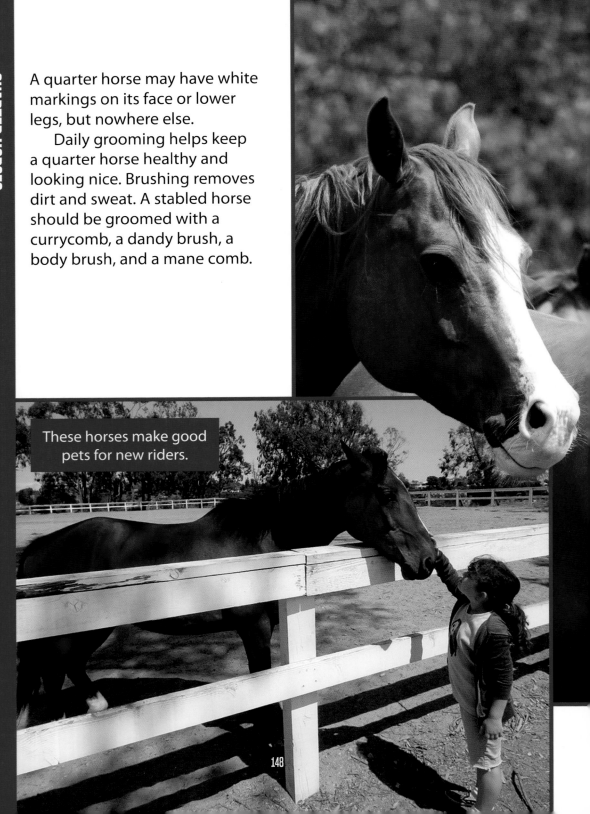

These horses make good pets for new riders.

The chestnut coloration is the most common color among quarter horses.

WHAT MAKES THEM SPECIAL

In the 1800s, pioneers and settlers moved west. They took their quarter horses with them. The horses pulled wagons and plows. They were also good cow ponies. They had excellent instincts for herding cattle.

Quarter horses are very agile. They move quickly and can make fast turns, which helps them herd cattle.

Quarter horses often compete in rodeo events, such as roping. During this event, the horse gives chase to a calf while the rider attempts to lasso the calf.

Quarter horses are fast and move easily. They are known for the ability to start and stop quickly. Today, quarter horses are popular on ranches and in rodeos, races, and horse shows. Many owners also enjoy using their quarter horses for pleasure riding.

FOALS

A baby quarter horse is lanky. It should stand on its wobbly legs for the first time within an hour of being born. Soon, it starts drinking its mother's milk.

Within 24 hours, the foal can trot and gallop with its mother. It follows her by instinct. However, it will tire easily, so it needs a lot of rest.

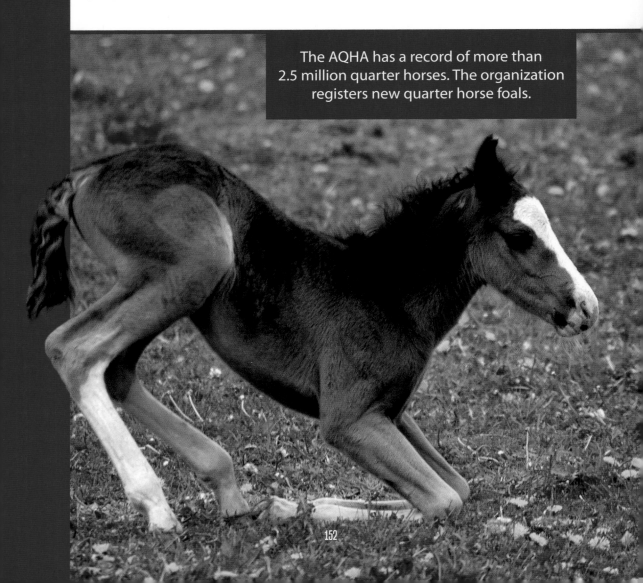

The AQHA has a record of more than 2.5 million quarter horses. The organization registers new quarter horse foals.

Foals will begin eating grass when they are about one week old.

TRAINING

Training a quarter horse requires skill and patience. A good trainer will teach a horse slowly. He or she will handle it gently but firmly.

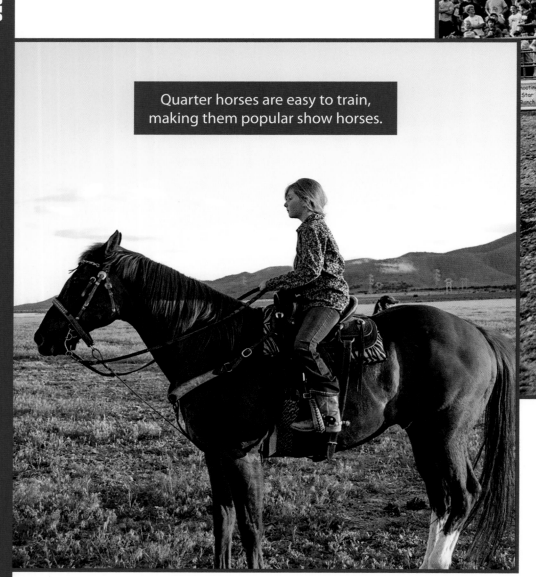

Quarter horses are easy to train, making them popular show horses.

A quarter horse shows off its agility during a barrel race.

A foal begins to learn soon after birth. At two years old, a quarter horse can be trained to wear a saddle. Like most horses, this breed learns through conditioning. Consistency is the most important thing to maintain when training a horse. A horse learns every time it is ridden.

SHETLAND PONIES

BREED HISTORY

The Shetland pony is one of today's smallest horse breeds. It originated in Scotland's Shetland Islands, where it served as a workhorse. Scotsmen used the ponies to haul peat for their fires.

Shetland ponies are one of the oldest horse breeds in the United Kingdom.

Shetland ponies are gentle and good with children.

In 1885, Shetland ponies arrived in North America. Within 50 years, a second Shetland pony breed emerged there. Today, that breed is known as the American Shetland pony. Though different, both Scottish and American Shetlands are popular with horse lovers.

APPEARANCE

The Scottish Shetland pony's features developed from its original surroundings. The Shetland Islands have harsh winter weather, so the pony's bushy mane and tail help block the wind. In winter, a double coat provides extra warmth. The pony sheds this thick hair in summer to reveal a smooth, shiny coat.

The Scottish Shetland pony has powerful shoulders and a short, wide back. Its legs are short and strong. The pony's small head features a broad forehead and muzzle. On average, Scottish Shetlands weigh about 400 to 450 pounds (180 to 200 kg). They can be 7 to 11.5 hands tall.

SHETLAND PONY SIZE

6 FEET
(1.8 M)

9 HANDS HIGH
(3 FEET / 0.9 M)

Shetland ponies start growing their winter coats earlier in the fall than most horses. They also shed their winter coats later in the spring.

American Shetlands can be taller than Scottish Shetlands.

The American Shetland looks more graceful than the Scottish Shetland. Its legs are long and fine. This breed has a smooth coat, yet it retains the thick Scottish mane and tail.

COLOR

Shetland ponies come in many colors. Common colors are bay, chestnut, black, gray, and dun. In addition, Scottish Shetlands are often dappled. A blue roan coat is also common.

Shetland ponies can have pinto coats.

A bay pony has a light to dark reddish-brown coat. Its points are black. A pony with a brown coat and the same color or lighter points is a chestnut. Black ponies have all black hairs unless they have markings. Markings are solid white patches on the head and the legs.

Many Shetland ponies are black or dark brown, but they can be other colors as well.

Shetland ponies should be brushed regularly to keep their coats healthy. Their hooves should also be checked and cleaned often.

A pony with white hairs on dark skin is a gray. A dun pony displays a light yellow to a dark tan coat. Its points are black or another dark color. A blue roan pony has black hairs mixed with white hairs.

With regular grooming, a Shetland's coat will stay clean and healthy. Owners should use a rubber currycomb and a body brush to remove dirt and dust. Then they should use a comb to help untangle the pony's thick mane and tail.

WHAT MAKES THEM SPECIAL

Scottish Shetland ponies are known for their small sizes and great strength. For their size, they are one of the strongest horse breeds. These ponies can pull twice their own body weight.

    With such power, these small ponies once worked in coal mines. In the 1840s, miners used strong Scottish Shetland ponies to haul coal through tight tunnels.

Despite their sizes, Shetland ponies are very strong. They can be used to pull carts and for farmwork.

Shetlands are friendly horses.

Shetlands make up for their small sizes with their big personalities. Some people think Shetlands are stubborn and strong willed. Yet they are actually bright, happy animals. When well trained, these ponies are easy to manage and eager to please.

FOALS

Like all horses, an adult female Shetland is called a mare. She mates with an adult male called a stallion. Then, the mare may become pregnant. After about 11 months, she gives birth to a foal.

After the foal is born, its mother licks it clean. Within an hour, the wobbly foal learns to stand. The newborn foal must quickly learn to nurse. For only a short time, the mare's milk has colostrum in it. Colostrum helps protect the foal from harmful diseases.

Foals are weak when they are born. They can get sick easily.

These ponies are known for their long lifespans. Some can live for more than 50 years.

After about six months, the foal is weaned. It will continue growing alongside other young horses. Most horses live 20 to 30 years. Healthy ponies generally live longer than larger horses.

TRAINING

The best time to begin training any pony is when it is young. Shetland ponies are quick learners. They may become bored with long, repetitive training. So, trainers give short lessons and teach ponies new skills one at a time.

Shetland ponies are easier to train when they are young.

Children are able to use Shetland ponies to compete in races.

Shetlands are athletic animals. Once they have completed basic training, they can be trained for driving a cart or riding. Many Shetlands also train for driving and jumping competitions. These versatile ponies offer horse lovers many fun options in a small package.

BREED HISTORY

The Thoroughbred horse is an impressive breed that started more than 300 years ago. Several Englishmen brought three Arabian horses to England from the Middle East. The first Thoroughbreds descended from these Arabians.

In 1730, the Thoroughbred horse arrived in North America. Then in 1894, the Jockey Club formed. This group maintains the American Stud Book. It documents all Thoroughbred breeding in North America.

Kentucky and Tennessee were among the first US states to establish interest in Thoroughbred breeding and racing.

Thoroughbred horses are a result of hundreds of years of selective breeding. Breeders paired their best mares with the best stallions to increase strength and stamina.

APPEARANCE

The Thoroughbred is a widely recognized horse breed. This beautiful animal takes many of its features from its Arabian relatives. The Thoroughbred has widely spaced, intelligent eyes and a delicate head. Its neck is long and graceful.

The Thoroughbred horse is a racing machine. It has a slim body with a short, curved back. Powerful muscles command all four of the horse's long legs.

Thoroughbred horses weigh about 1,000 to 1,200 pounds (450 to 900 kg). On average, they stand about 16 hands high.

THOROUGHBRED HORSE SIZE

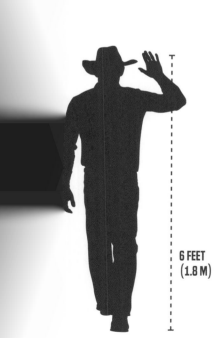

6 FEET
(1.8 M)

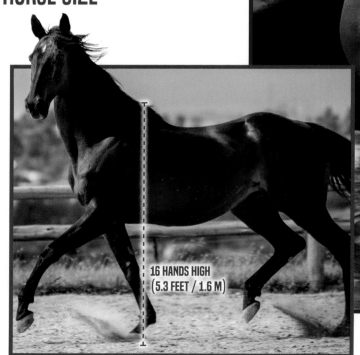

16 HANDS HIGH
(5.3 FEET / 1.6 M)

Thoroughbreds have long back legs.

COLOR

Common colors for Thoroughbreds include bay, chestnut, gray, and black. Bay horses have light to dark reddish-brown coats with black points. Chestnut horses have brown coats and points.

Gray horses are born with dark hair that often turns white with age. Black horses have all black coats and points. They can also have white markings.

Thoroughbreds are mostly solid in color.

Thoroughbreds tend to be dark in color, ranging from bay to black.

Markings are solid white patches of hair found on the head and the legs. They can be seen on any Thoroughbred horse. Common head markings are a star, a stripe, a blaze, a snip, and a bald face. Leg markings include ankles, socks, and stockings.

Thoroughbreds can have white markings on their faces like stars (*left*) and blazes (*right*).

WHAT MAKES THEM SPECIAL

For more than 300 years, breeders have been perfecting the Thoroughbred's racing qualities. Today, these horses combine amazing speed and great strength. Secretariat and Man o' War are among the most famous Thoroughbred racehorses.

During a race, Thoroughbreds can gallop at more than 40 miles per hour (64 kmh). A Thoroughbred's single stride can cover more than 20 feet (6 m) of ground.

Secretariat won the Triple Crown in 1973. He was very far ahead of the competition in the Belmont Stakes race.

Thoroughbreds are more than just powerful racehorses. These animals also excel at jumping and other sports. Thoroughbreds are sometimes crossbred with other horse types to improve those breeds.

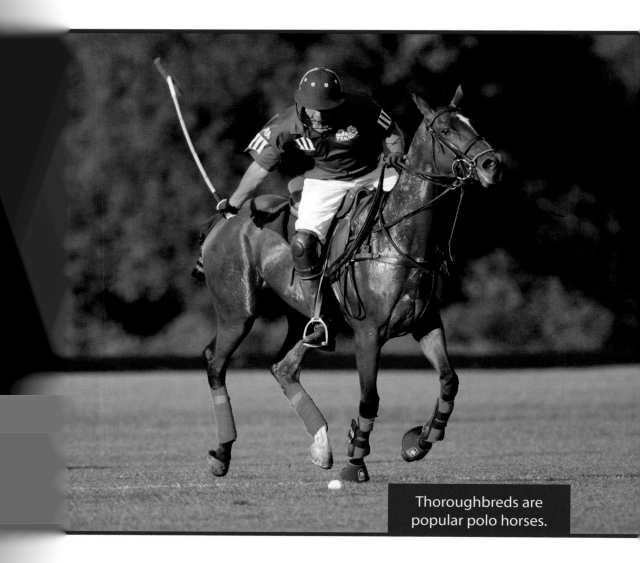

Thoroughbreds are popular polo horses.

FOALS

Breeding Thoroughbreds is serious business. Breeders are careful to mate the best parents they can. Thoroughbred organizations have decided that all these horses turn one year older on the same day each year: January 1. This is even true if a foal is born on December 31. In this case, when the foal is really just one day old, the Thoroughbred organizations will recognize it as one year old on January 1.

Sometimes, people use the term *thoroughbred* to mean purebred.

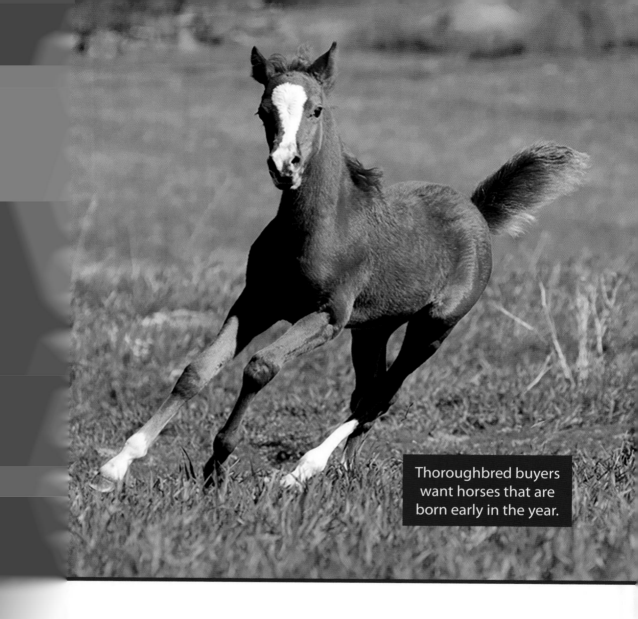

Thoroughbred buyers want horses that are born early in the year.

Horses of the same age race against each other. American breeders want their Thoroughbred foals born as soon after January 1 as possible. That's because horse buyers don't usually want to buy horses born later in the year. These horses are too young to successfully compete against older horses in the same age group. If a horse is born soon after January 1, it has time to develop and train. Most Thoroughbred horses go on to live for 20 to 30 years.

TRAINING

A Thoroughbred horse begins training for its racing career as a yearling. At this young age, it learns to follow commands, change pace, wear tack, and be ridden. Then, it trains on a racetrack with a jockey. As a two-year-old, a Thoroughbred horse can enter its first race. Racing events are exciting and competitive.

Jockeys slowly introduce young Thoroughbreds to riding gear. The horse learns to adjust to the rider's weight in a stall before walking along a track.

Justify became the 13th Triple Crown winner in 2018.

Only three-year-old Thoroughbreds can compete to win the Triple Crown, which is a title earned by a horse for winning the Kentucky Derby, the Preakness Stakes, and the Belmont Stakes races. This means a horse gets just one chance to become the winner. Only 13 horses have achieved this feat.

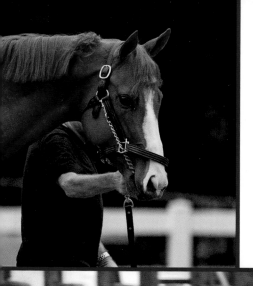

By the time Thoroughbreds are five years old, many are retired from racing. However, they can be retrained for other purposes. These beautiful horses continue to thrill horse lovers every day.

Horse racing is a serious business.

HORSE CARE

Taking proper care of horses prevents many health problems. An owner is responsible for providing his or her animal with a dry home in a stable or a barn. The owner is also responsible for knowing how to properly care for his or her specific breed of horse.

Generally, a horse's stall should be clean and have plenty of fresh air. The horse should also have comfortable bedding to lie upon. Bedding can be wood shavings, straw, or shredded hemp spread over the floor.

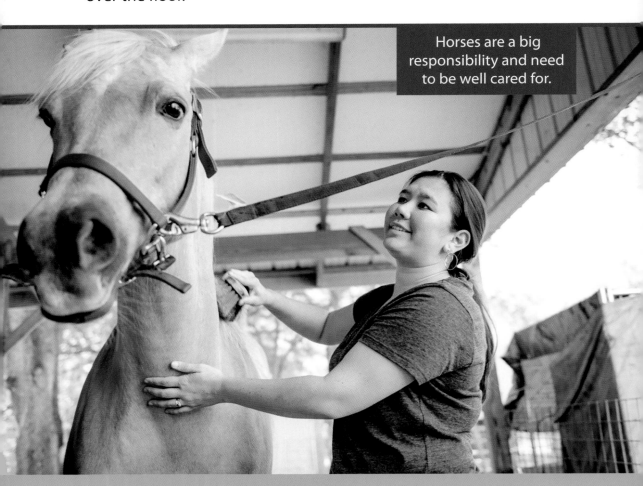

Horses are a big responsibility and need to be well cared for.

Items can get stuck in a horse's hooves and injure the horse. That's why it's important to check a horse's hooves and clean them.

Grooming helps keep a horse healthy and its coat looking nice. Brushing removes dirt from the coat. A stabled horse should be groomed daily with a currycomb, a body brush, and a mane and tail comb.

A horse's feet should be checked daily. People use hoof picks to remove dirt and stones from the feet. The hooves will usually need trimming every four to six weeks. Also, owners should check that the horseshoes are in good shape, if the horse wears them.

Horses should see a veterinarian at least once a year. He or she can check the horse to make sure it is healthy. The veterinarian can also float a horse's teeth as needed. Filing down any uneven teeth helps prevent chewing problems.

Horses also need proper gear. A horse's equipment is called tack. Tack should fit well and be kept clean. This way, it will not irritate the horse or cause other problems.

Saddles come in two types. A western saddle has wide stirrups and a horn. It is best for working horses. An English saddle is flatter and lighter than a Western saddle. It is used in racing, hunting, and fence jumping.

A saddle is set on top of a saddle pad. The pad absorbs sweat from the horse's back. It also protects the horse's back and sides from the rubbing of the saddle.

A bridle is used to control a horse. It is made of leather straps that fit over the horse's head. A bit attaches to the straps. The bit is a piece of metal that fits in the horse's mouth. Reins are attached to the bit.

Spurs and whips are used to give the horse signals. But these items should only be used by a trained rider.

It's important to have the proper equipment for your horse.

GLOSSARY

bald face
A wide, white marking covering most of an animal's face.

blaze
A usually white, broad stripe down the center of an animal's face.

coronet
A white marking on the band around the top of a horse's hoof.

dappled
Marked with small spots of a different color or shade from the background.

forelock
A tuft of hair growing above the forehead.

halter
A rope or strap for leading or restraining an animal.

hock
A joint in a hind leg of a four-legged animal. A hock is similar to a knee joint, except that it bends backward.

peat
A piece of heavy turf cut and dried for use as fuel.

pony trekking
The act of riding a pony through the countryside.

snip
A white marking between a horse's nostrils.

steppe
Any large, flat plain without trees.

wean
To accustom an animal to eat food other than its mother's milk.

withers
The highest part of a horse's back.

TO LEARN MORE

FURTHER READINGS

Clutton-Brock, Juliet. *Horse*. DK Publishing, 2016.

De la Bédoyère, Camilla. *Horses and Ponies*. Gareth Stevens, 2016.

Horses: The Definitive Catalog of Horse and Pony Breeds. Scholastic, 2019.

ONLINE RESOURCES

To learn more about horses, please visit **abdobooklinks.com** or scan this QR code. These links are routinely monitored and updated to provide the most current information available.

INDEX

PHOTO CREDITS

ABDOBOOKS.COM

Published by Abdo Publishing, a division of ABDO, PO Box 398166, Minneapolis, Minnesota 55439. Copyright © 2021 by Abdo Consulting Group, Inc. International copyrights reserved in all countries. No part of this book may be reproduced in any form without written permission from the publisher. Abdo Reference™ is a trademark and logo of Abdo Publishing.

Printed in the United States of America, North Mankato, Minnesota.
082020
012021

Editor: Alyssa Krekelberg
Series Designer: Colleen McLaren

LIBRARY OF CONGRESS CONTROL NUMBER: 2019954299

PUBLISHER'S CATALOGING-IN-PUBLICATION DATA

Names: Pembroke, Ethan, author.
Title: The horse encyclopedia for kids / by Ethan Pembroke
Description: Minneapolis, Minnesota : Abdo Publishing, 2021 | Series: Encyclopedias for kids | Includes online resources and index.
Identifiers: ISBN 9781532193019 (lib. bdg.) | ISBN 9781098210915 (ebook)
Subjects: LCSH: Horses--Juvenile literature. | Horses--Behavior--Juvenile literature. | Reference materials-- Juvenile literature.
Classification: DDC 599.72--dc23